Coloring Books for Adults

100% ORIGINAL

MANDALAS

By: Julia Brockmann

ISBN-13 978-1517082178

PUBLISHERS NOTES

Disclaimer

Published by InfoEbooksOnline.com

Paperback Edition

Manufactured in the United States of America

Try out your color ideas here:

Try out your color ideas here:

Try out your color ideas here:

Try out your color ideas here:

Try out your color ideas here:

Try out your color ideas here:

Try out your color ideas here:

Try out your color ideas here:

Try out your color ideas here:

Try out your color ideas here:

Try out your color ideas here:

Try out your color ideas here:

Try out your color ideas here:

Try out your color ideas here:

Try out your color ideas here:

Try out your color ideas here:

Try out your color ideas here:

Try out your color ideas here:

Try out your color ideas here:

Try out your color ideas here:

Try out your color ideas here:

Try out your color ideas here:

Try out your color ideas here:

Try out your color ideas here:

Try out your color ideas here:

Try out your color ideas here:

Try out your color ideas here:

Try out your color ideas here:

Try out your color ideas here:

Try out your color ideas here:

Try out your color ideas here:

Try out your color ideas here:

Try out your color ideas here:

Adult Coloring Books -
Julia Brockmann

https://www.createspace.com

Other Coloring Books by InfoEbooksOnline

INFOEBOOKSONLINE

InfoEbooksOnline is a well known publishing company which specializes in lifestyle books of many kinds for both adult and children.

Their philosophy is:

Work hard and enjoy life through activities that replenish the body and the soul.

Paperback products can be sourced through

CreateSpace.com

www.ingramcontent.com/pod-product-compliance
Lightning Source LLC
Chambersburg PA
CBHW052040280526
45791CB00010B/3019